To live freely

within our

chosen boundaries

is a way as

beautiful and fair

as our land.

America the Beautiful – Signs of Learning®

— *For the First People* —

Registered Title: Murray David Harwich III

Original Poem by Katharine Lee Bates

Text ©2015 Mary Belle Harwich

Illustrations © 2015 Robert Wapahi,

Photograph Nora Moore Lloyd

Printed in the United States

Printed in the United States

Published Frankfort, KY

Book Designs by Marjorie Snelson Design

ISBN 978-0-9888972 2-9

Library of Congress Control Number: 2015911289

To order printed books: www.amazon.com

America the Beautiful
Signs of Learning®

Original Poem by Katharine Lee Bates

Text by Mary Belle Harwich

Illustrations by Robert Wapahi

O beautiful

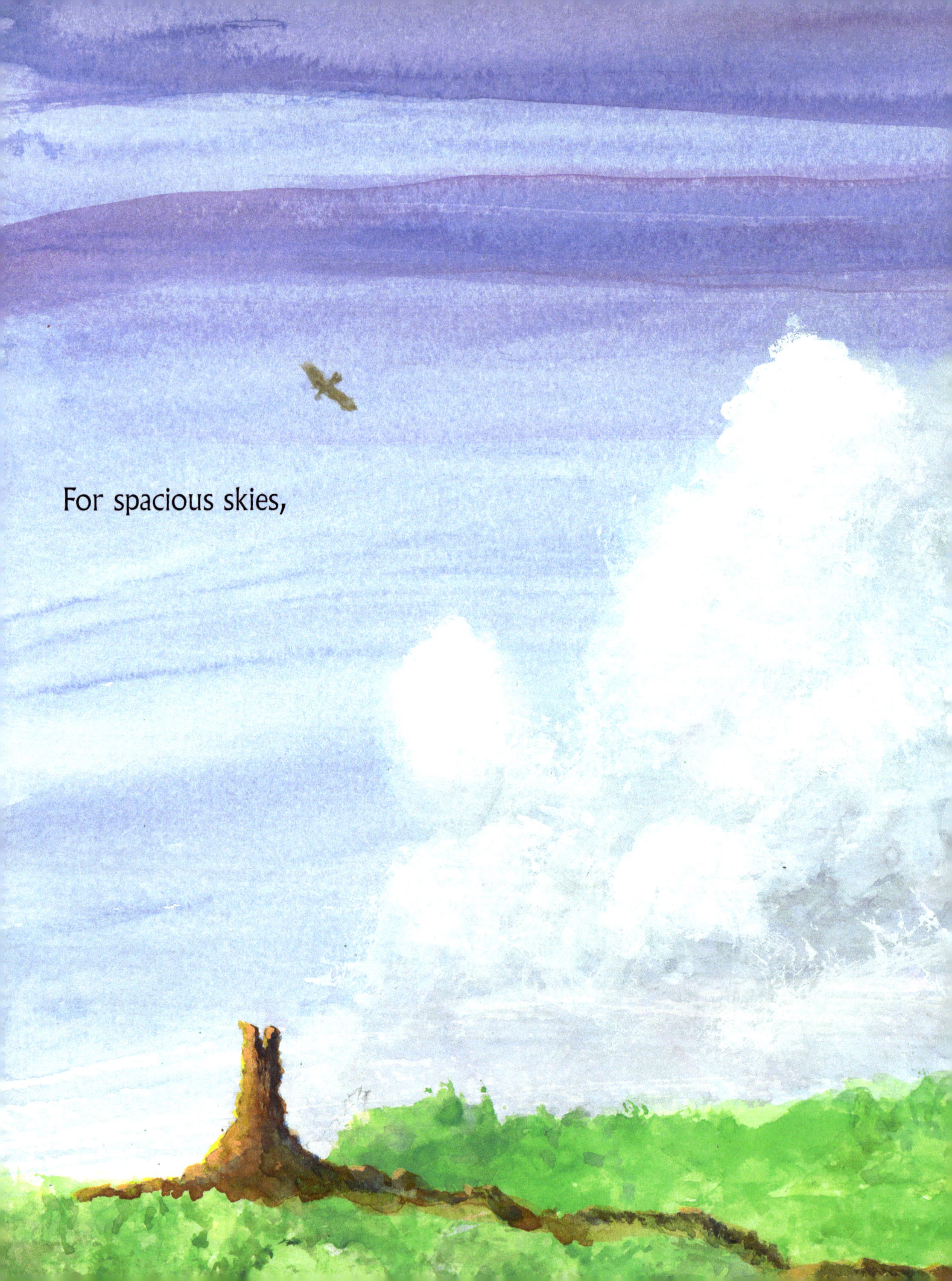

For spacious skies,

For amber waves of grain,

For purple mountain majesties

Above the fruited plain!

America!

America!

God shed His grace on thee

And crown thy good

with brotherhood

From sea

to shining sea!

Signs of Learning

American Sign Language

Beautiful . . . . 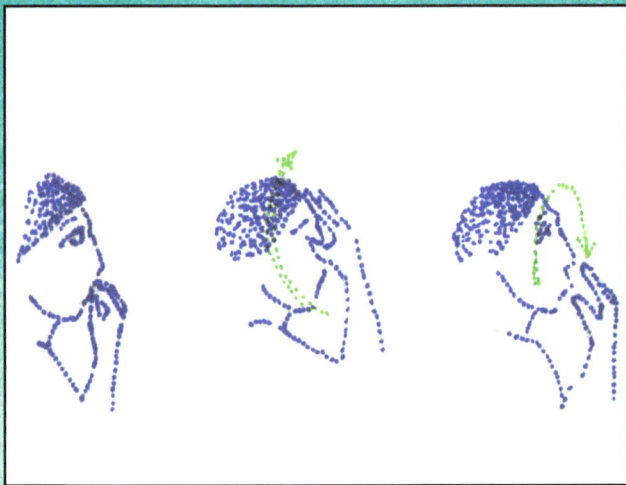 B E A U T I F U L

For . . . . 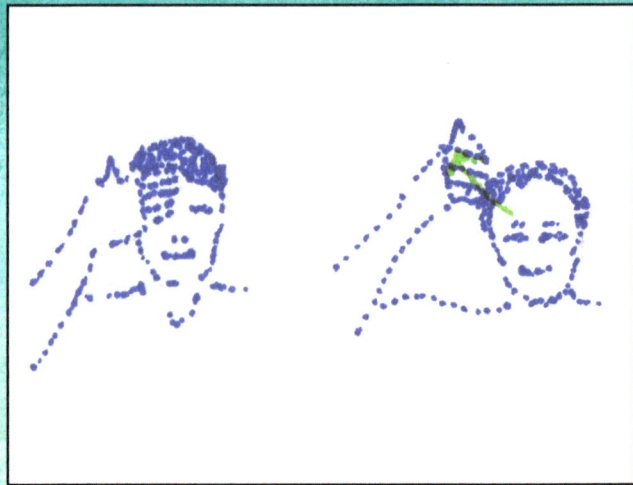 F O R

Spacious . . . . 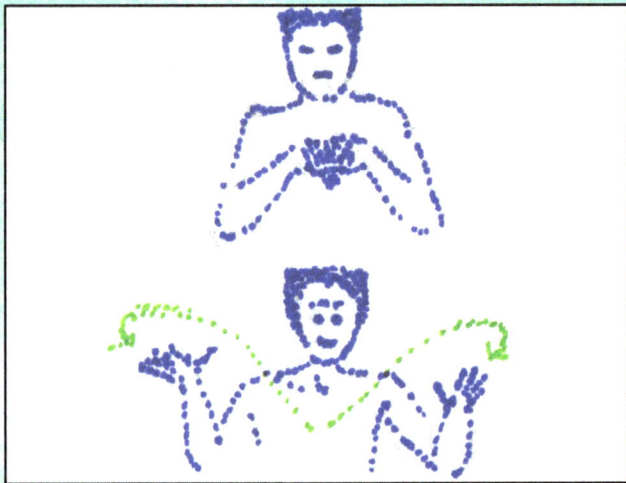 S P A C I O U S

Skies . . . . 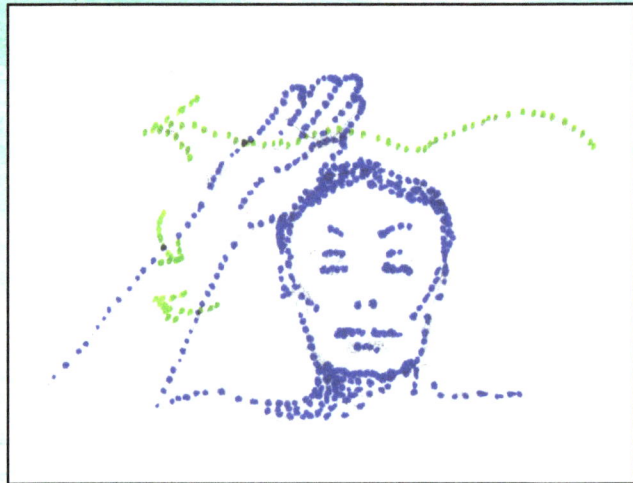 S K I E S

For . . . . 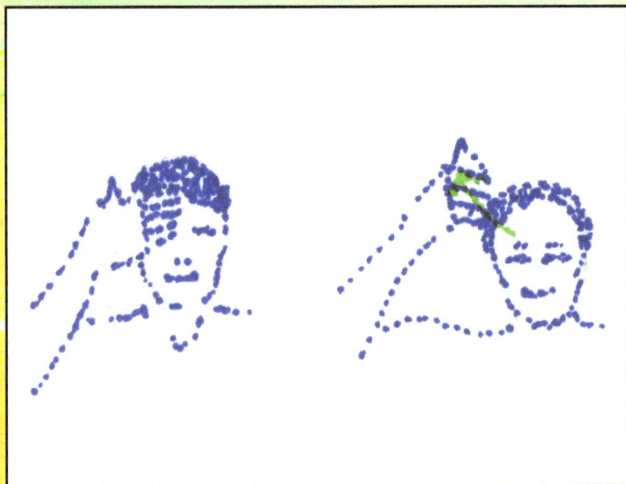 F O R

Waves . . . . 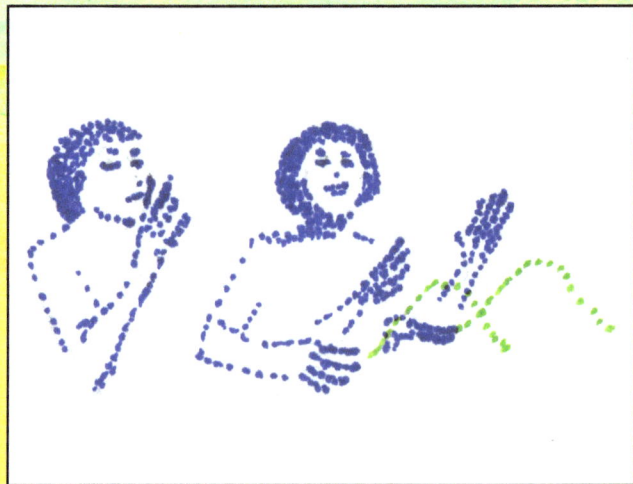 W A V E S

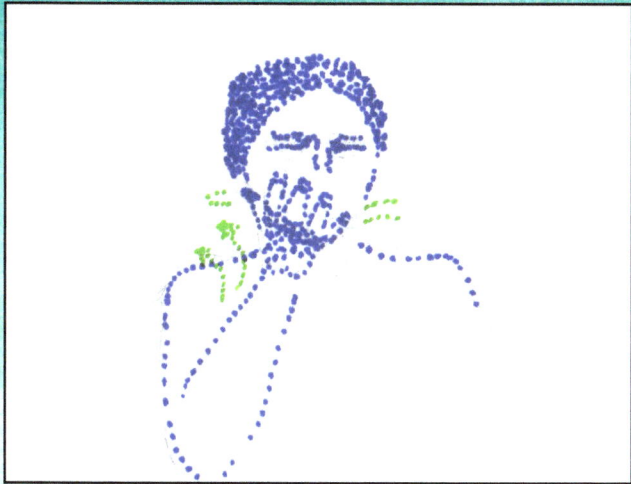

Grain . . . . 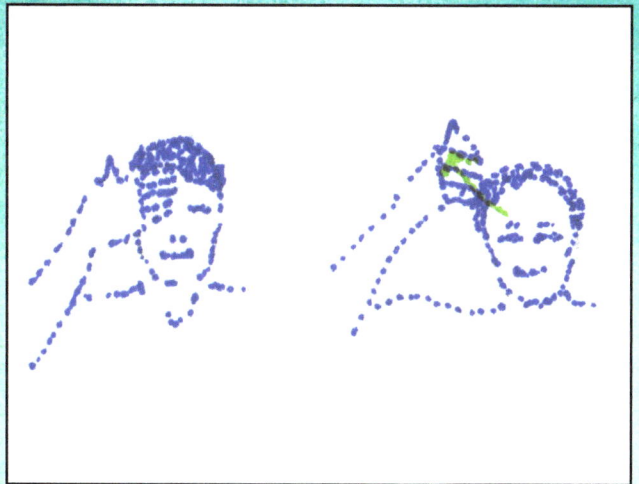 G R A I N

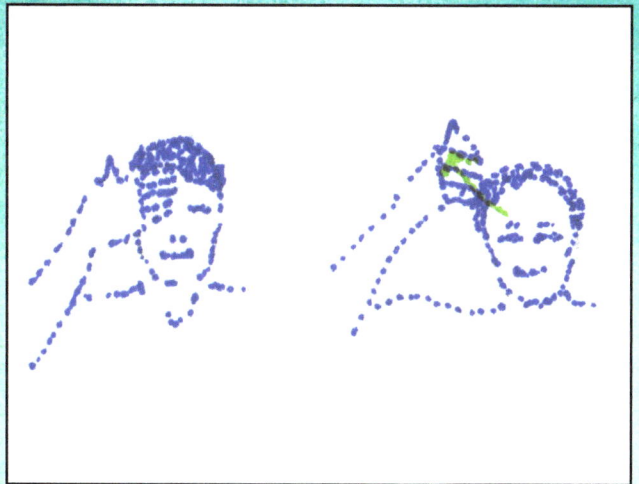

For . . . . 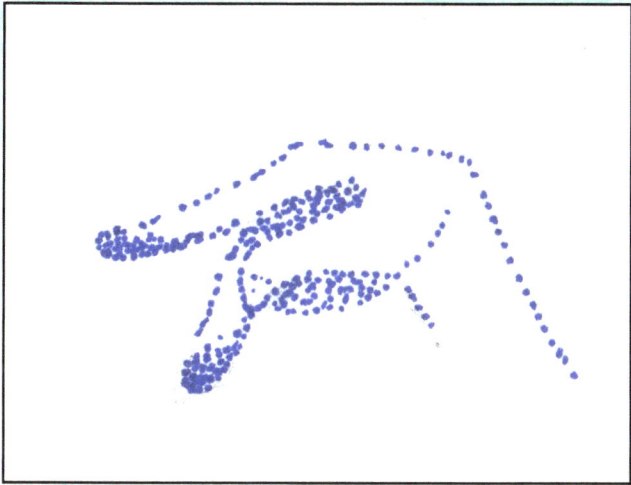 F O R

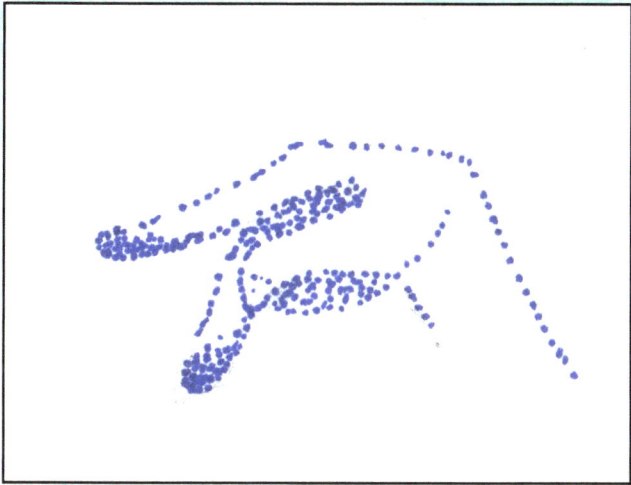

Purple . . . .  P U R P L E

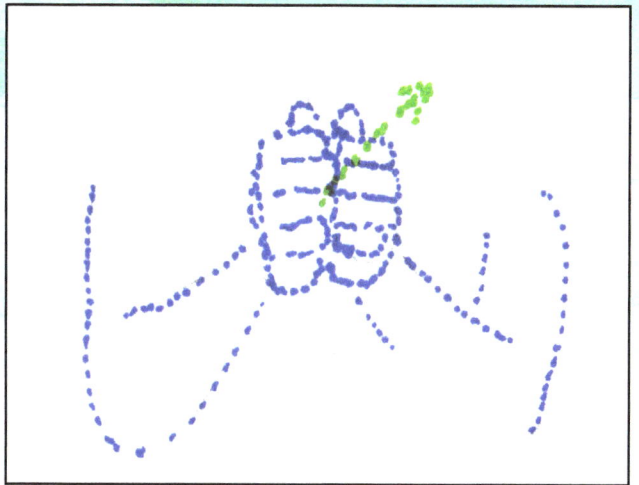

Mountain . . . . .  M O U N T A I N

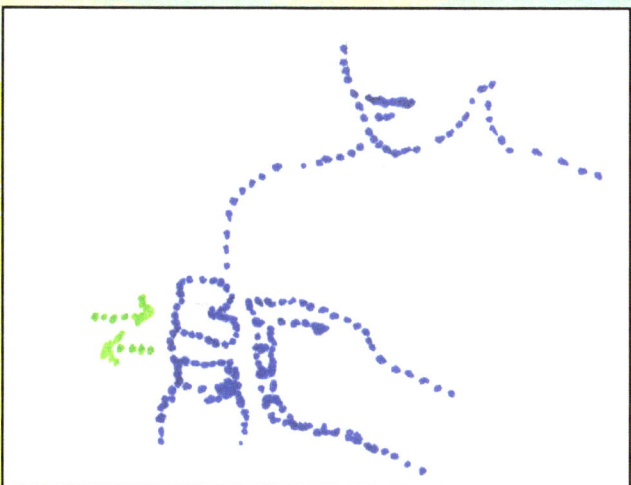

Majesties . .  M A J E S T I E S

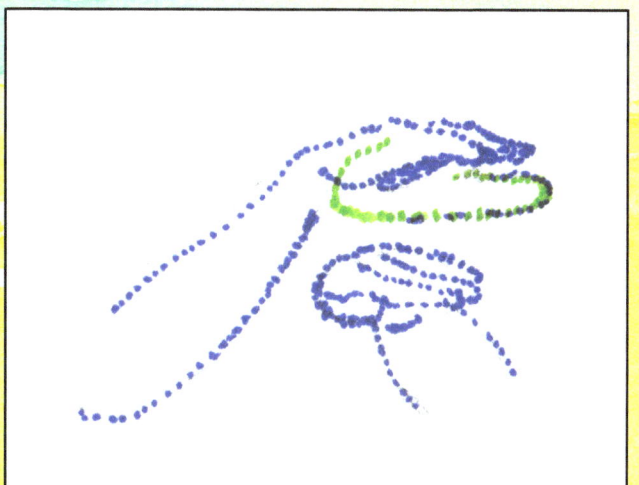

Above . . . .  A B O V E

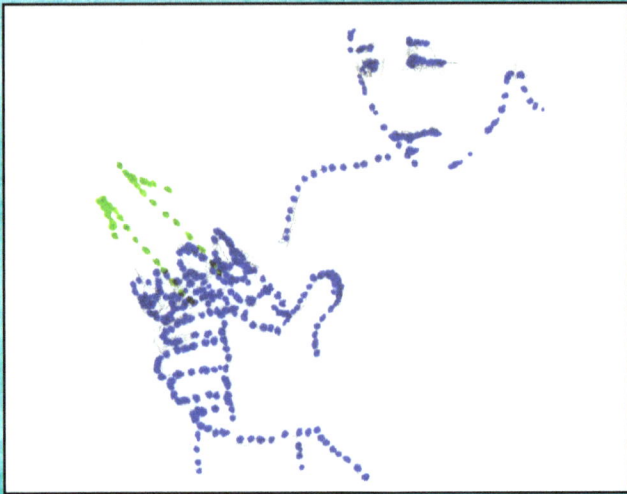

Fruited . . . .

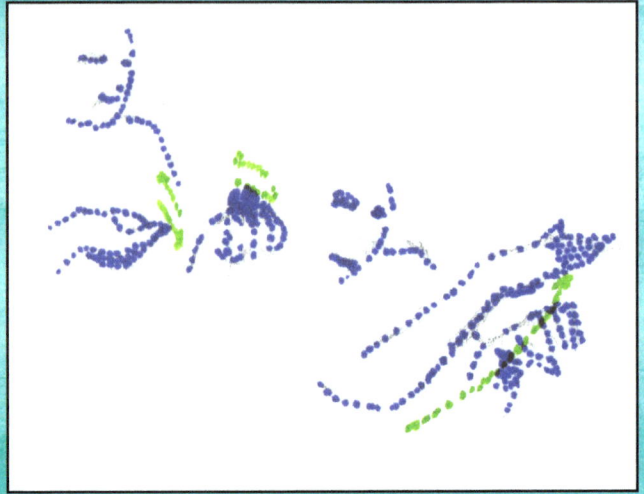

Plain . . . .

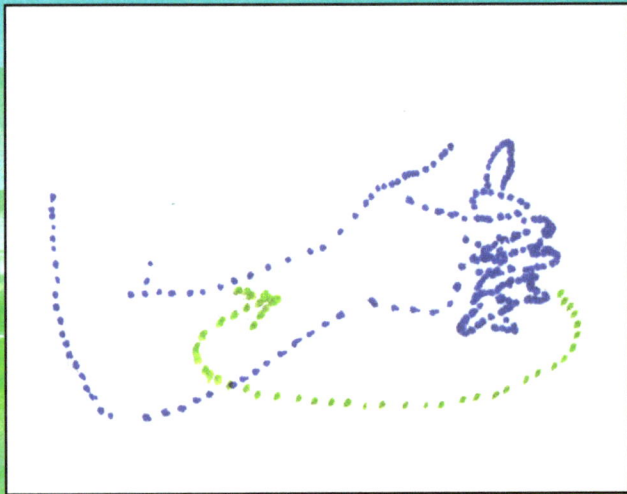

America . . . .

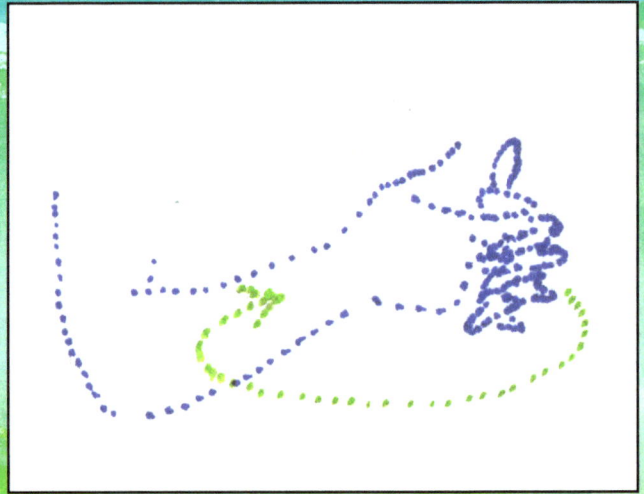

America . . . .

God . . . .

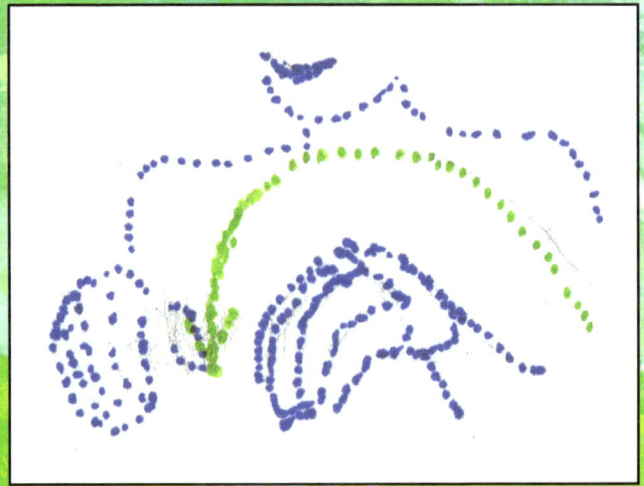

Shed . . . .

Grace. . . . .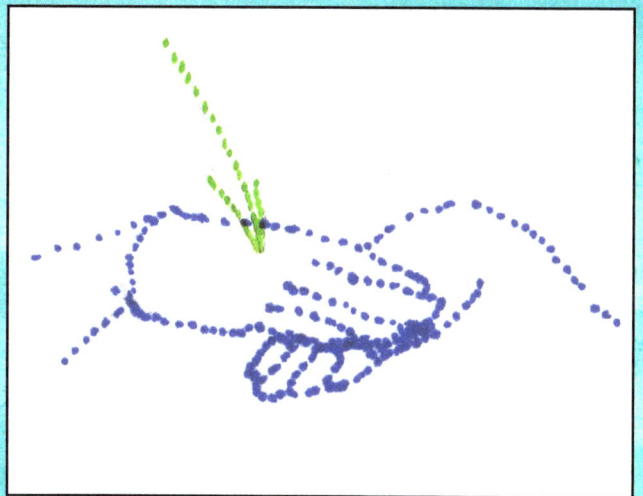

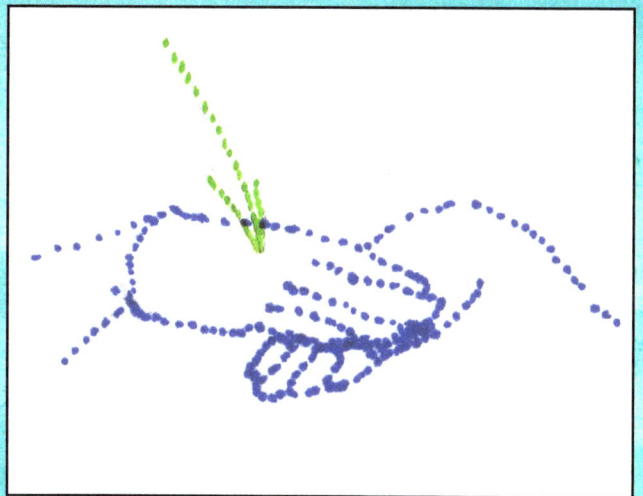

On. . . . .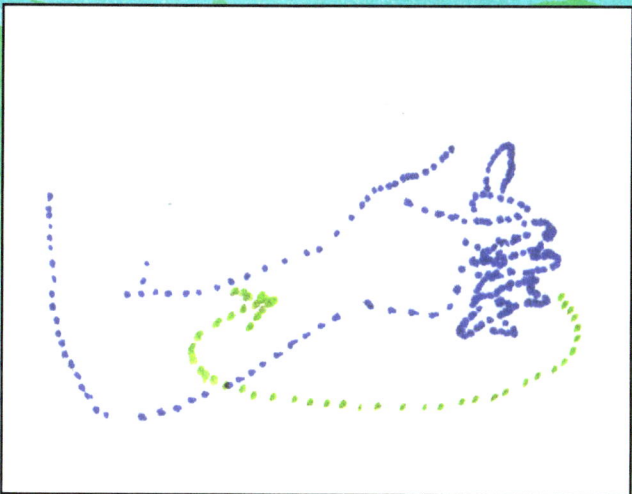

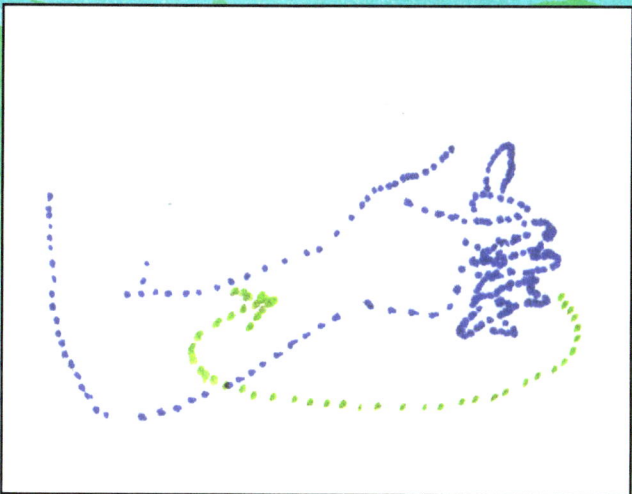

Thee (America) . . .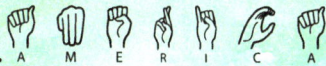

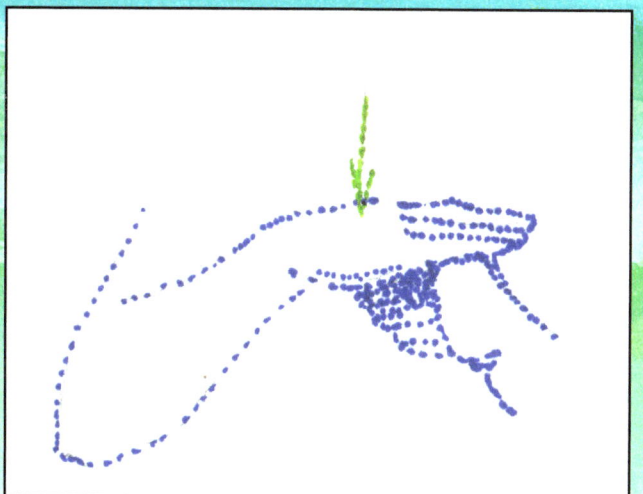

Crown. . . . .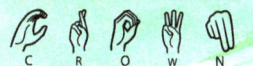

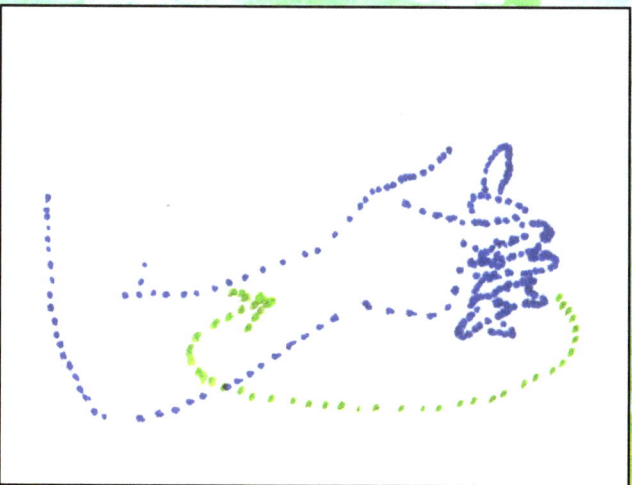

Thy. . . . .

Good. . . . .

With . . . .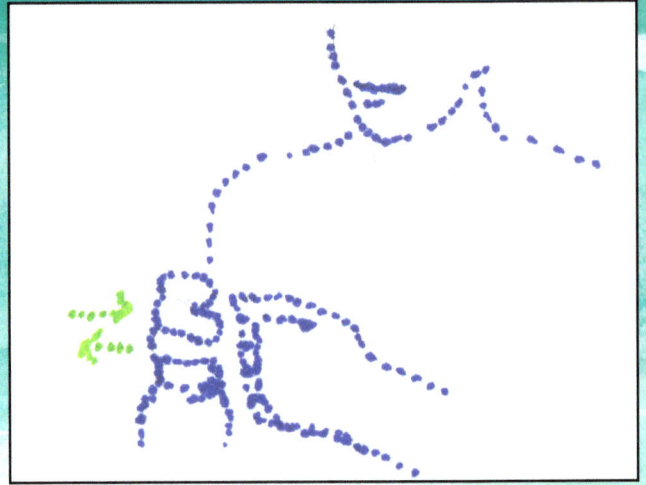

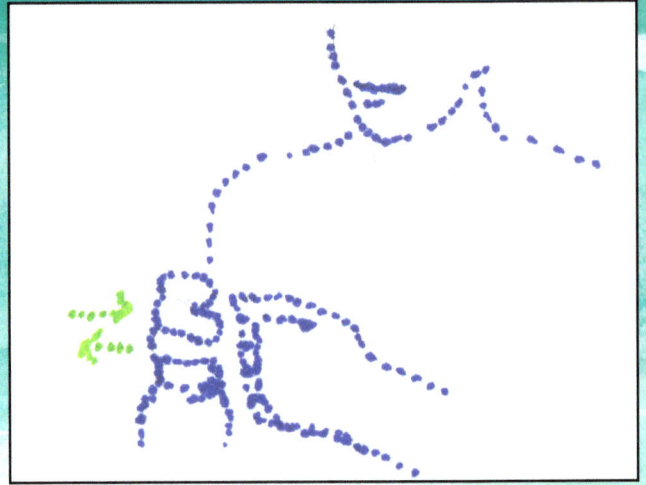

Brotherhood . .

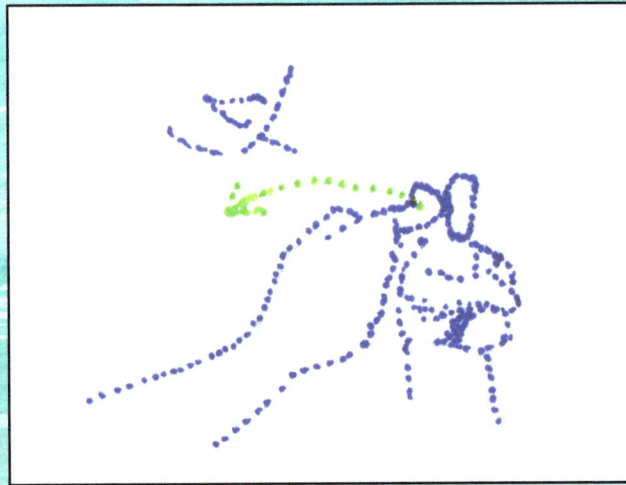

America . . . .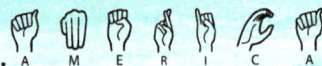

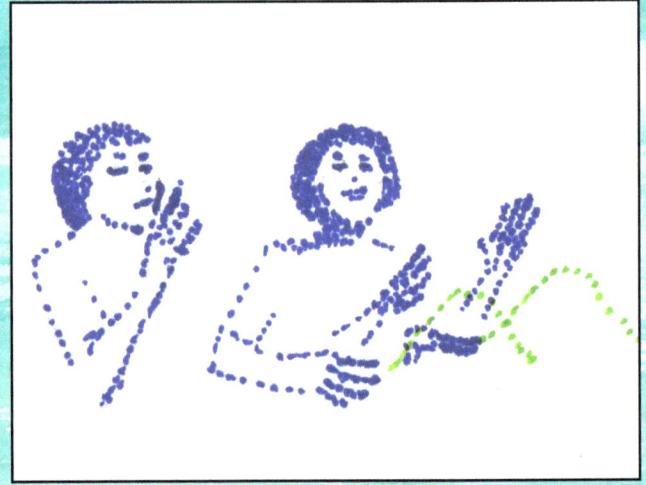

Sea . . . .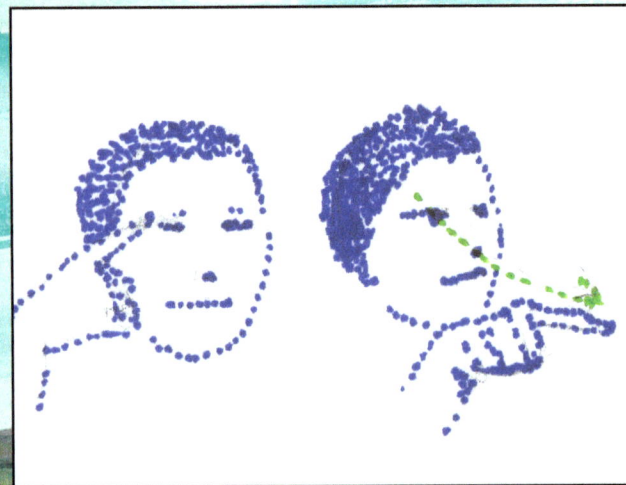

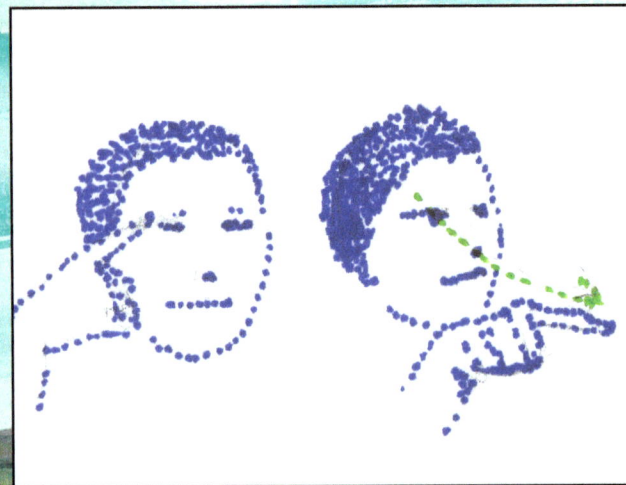

To . . . .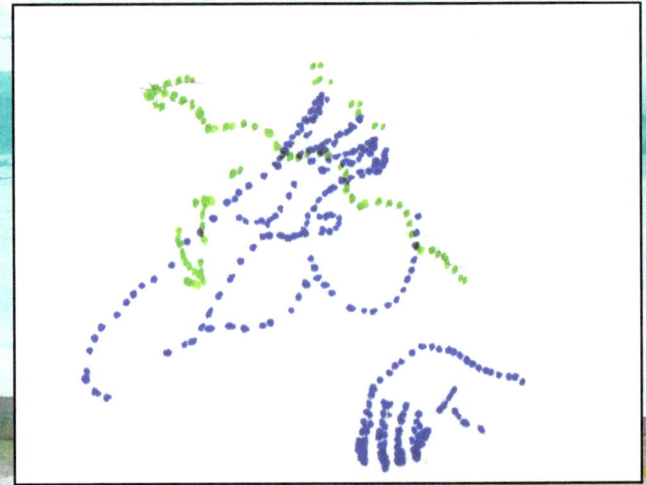

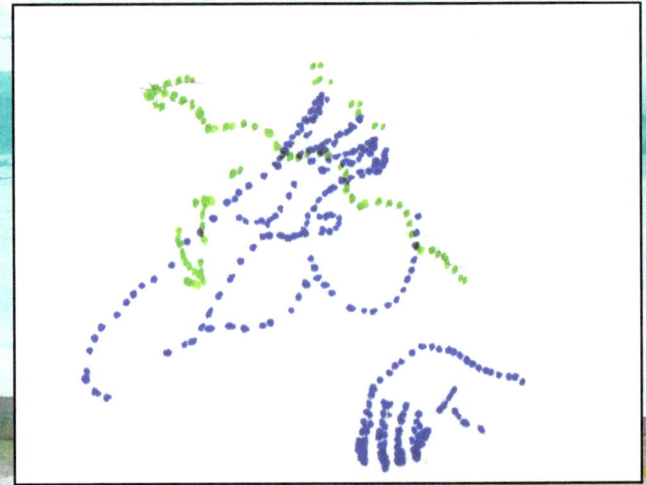

Shining . . . .

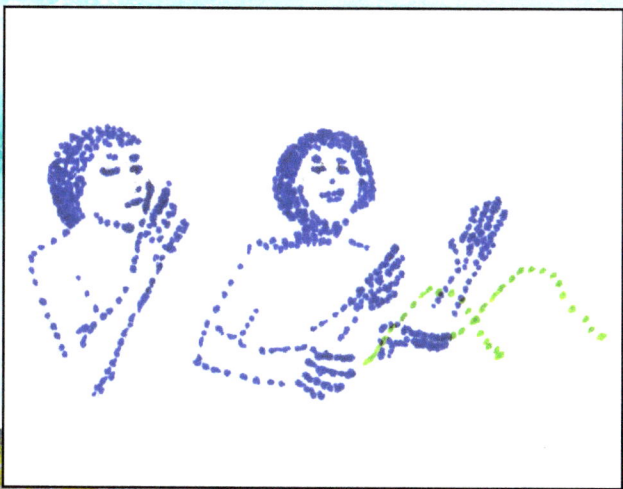

Sea . . . .

Robert Wapahi, Dakota, was born in 1945 on the Santee Indian Reservation in South Dakota. Pen and ink has become his favorite medium with oils coming in at a close second. Of note, most compositions are horizontal or landscape, which is only fitting for someone from the Great Plains. Robert is also an accomplished musician and traditional storyteller. His work is represented in private collections and he has participated in group exhibitions and solo shows.

One land

One people.